Kevin Armento

DEVIL WITH THE BLUE DRESS

OBERON BOOKS
LONDON

WWW.OBERONBOOKS.COM

First published in 2018 by Oberon Books Ltd
521 Caledonian Road, London N7 9RH
Tel: +44 (0) 20 7607 3637 / Fax: +44 (0) 20 7607 3629
e-mail: info@oberonbooks.com
www.oberonbooks.com

A catalogue record for this book is available from the British Library.

PB ISBN: 9781786824936
E ISBN: 9781786824943

Cover design by David Ralf

Characters

HILLARY, 40s

MONICA, 20s

BETTY, 50s

CHELSEA, late teens

LINDA, 40s

and

THE SAXOPHONIST, male, any age

NOTE

BETTY is African-American, the others any ethnicity.

TIME

Article One: Perjury
January - August 1998
and
July 1995 - February 1997

Article Two: Obstruction of Justice
August 1998
and
February 1997 - August 1998

HOW IT PLAYS

Smooth and seductive. Lots of stage magic.
Traveling through time fluidly, as memory does.

CHELSEA, LINDA, and BETTY play several other
characters throughout, including BILL. These
transformations can be swift and suggestive, and
shouldn't require any significant costume changes.

NOTE ON TEXT

/ indicates point of interruption for the next speaker

– indicates self-interruption

… indicates speech that trails off

Five spaces indicates a beat of   articulation

"One of my husband's favorite southern sayings is, 'If you find a turtle on a fence post, it didn't get there by accident.'"

Hillary Rodham Clinton

Article One: Perjury

A playing space suggestive of the Oval Office.

THE SAXOPHONIST is there, playing solo improvisation: Lee Konitz, Sonny Rollins, Steve Lacy doing Monk.

We listen for a while. Until we're transfixed by the music. Until we aren't paying attention to anything else.

It's then that HILLARY appears.

HILLARY: Things I like about the theater:
Spectacle. Compelling narrative. Likeable characters.
All the things I'm told I lack.

>   *Beat.*

And if politics is the art of the possible, theater is the art of the impossible.
I like that.

>   *She looks around the space.*

This play, for instance…
My play…
It exists in the space between awake and asleep. Do you know it? Where you can't tell if the things racing through your head are thoughts   or dreams? So you can sort of control them…but sort of can't? That's where we are.

Being that kind of space, things aren't totally realistic. It's dimly lit. It's set to music. And it's where memory lives…

LINDA AS BILL: *(Off.)* Honey, you're going to hear about a story today. Intern. Affair. Cover-up.

HILLARY: Memory that's deeply hidden. Memory I've never traveled down…until tonight.

As I say, I don't know if it's in thought or in dream, but tonight this particular memory is beckoning.

Like a good play, it is – impossibly – sucking me in…

1

> *She steps into the memory and LINDA, BETTY and*
> *CHELSEA appear.*

HILLARY: These are the other characters. There's Chelsea, my daughter. Betty, Bill's secretary. And Linda…a Republican. I can see them, just as they were then. I can hear them. And through them, I can hear him:

LINDA AS BILL: Honey, you're gonna hear a story today. Intern. Affair. Cover-up.

HILLARY: This is how the play begins.

LINDA AS BILL: It just went up on some guy's website, Drudge something, so no one's gonna take it seriously – but didn't want you to be surprised.

BETTY: And were you surprised?

> *HILLARY looks at BETTY.*
>
> *BETTY looks at HILLARY.*

HILLARY: Let's see…

CHELSEA: January 20th, 1998.

BETTY: You're in the White House residence.

HILLARY: We're coming to the end of our fifth year in office. It's ten days until the State of the Union and we Democrats, we the fiscal irresponsibles, are about to propose the first balanced budget in three decades and use the word surplus with a straight face; we've signed family and medical leave, welfare reform, and the most sweeping gun control in a generation; we're building a bridge to the twenty-first century, unleashing the internet – and along with it the biggest economic boom in American history – and doing all of this while keeping the country out of war.

CHELSEA: And…

HILLARY: And… Flowers, Foster, Troopergate, Travelgate, Filegate, five rounds of Whitewater testimony and about to be dragged in for a sixth, and year four of the Paula Jones lawsuit. That's the two-step we'd been navigating: undeniable progress, met with relentless attempts by our enemies to create scandal. No evidence for any of them, to be sure, but round-the-clock coverage made possible by a fun new innovation called cable news. So no, Betty – not surprised.

LINDA: And how do you respond?

HILLARY looks at LINDA.

LINDA looks at HILLARY.

HILLARY: I sit up in our bed

LINDA: your bed in the White House

HILLARY: and I meet his look

LINDA: and you say

HILLARY: Let's get to work.

A flurry of music.

CHELSEA appears on a phone call.

CHELSEA: Hey Mom.

HILLARY: Hey did I wake you? I know it's / early over there…

CHELSEA: No it's fine, I'm about to go to class.

Off-phone.

Shh!

HILLARY: What'd you say /

CHELSEA: Nothing, what's up?

HILLARY: Listen, there's going to be something in the news today…

CHELSEA: *(Really annoyed.)* Aw man. / Serious?

HILLARY: I know, Dad just told me.

CHELSEA: What is it this time?

HILLARY: It's about a woman.

CHELSEA: The Paula Jones thing?

HILLARY: No, it's a new one, it's about someone who worked here.

CHELSEA: In the White House? God they're relentless. Who is it?

HILLARY: Some former intern. But don't worry about it, okay? Just wanted you to have a heads-up.

CHELSEA: *(Whispered off-phone.)* Yes it's my mom, shut up!

HILLARY: Who's there with you?

CHELSEA: Just my stupid friend. Are you guys ok?

HILLARY: Yeah we're fine, everything's good.

(Allowing some pride.) I got child care into the speech.

CHELSEA: In the State of the Union? That's amazing!

HILLARY: Yeah.

CHELSEA: Dad said you're kicking ass on it.

HILLARY: We'll see, I'm not getting hopes up after health care.

CHELSEA: That wasn't your fault.

HILLARY: Yes it was /

CHELSEA: That's not / true.

HILLARY: It was, but it's okay. This bill's going better.

CHELSEA: Good. Hey did you say that story's coming out today?

HILLARY: Yeah. It's just on a website, so shouldn't even...

CHELSEA: Yeah. Thanks.

HILLARY: You're going to class?

CHELSEA: Harlem Ren –

She has an abrupt fit of laughter off-phone.

Oh my god!

Back to phone.

Harlem Ren/aissance.

HILLARY: Ok what is going on over there?

CHELSEA: Nothing! Hon/estly.

HILLARY: Do you have a boy over?

CHELSEA: Mom!

HILLARY: And you thought you couldn't have a normal college experience.

CHELSEA: Oh super normal, excuse me while the Secret Service escorts me to class.

HILLARY: Stanford's turning you into such a smartass. I love it. Alright, I'm gonna –

CHELSEA: Wait, did we know her?

HILLARY: Who?

CHELSEA: The woman. What's her name?

> *More music as MONICA appears and the scene with CHELSEA dissipates.*
>
> *MONICA looks at HILLARY.*
>
> *HILLARY looks back.*

HILLARY: Why are you here?

MONICA: Why shouldn't I be?

HILLARY: It's my play.

> *MONICA looks around the space.*

MONICA: Don't you think all this is probably about me anyway?

HILLARY: That's just what I'd imagine you'd think.

MONICA: I think you want to know how it started for me.

HILLARY: I know how it / started.

MONICA: No you don't.

> *They share a look.*

MONICA: Doesn't seem fair if we only hear it from your perspective, does it?

HILLARY: Fairness isn't a theme of this play.

MONICA: *(To the others.)* What do you all think?

> *They look amongst themselves, confused.*

CHELSEA: I'd like to know.

MONICA looks at her. Then looks back at HILLARY.

MONICA: Doesn't every good play need an antagonist?

HILLARY looks at her a few beats. Considers.

HILLARY: Yours starts in an office.

MONICA: No. Before that. It starts at an arrival ceremony...

An arrival ceremony comes to life.

BETTY: July 27, 1995...

CHELSEA: You're on the South Lawn of the White House...

MONICA looks out at us.

MONICA: SorryI'mShyAllOfASudden.

She shakes it out.

It's a couple weeks into my internship, and the thing I'm quickly noticing is how much ritual there is in this place – the White House, not the theater, although theater has some weird shit too. But like when a foreign leader visits like this? It's incredibly precise:

She looks to LINDA, BETTY and CHELSEA for help, and they bring to life a state visit for her...

The South Lawn is decked out with a marching band, and people in colonial costumes. Very Main Street Disneyland. The news cameras are all setting up, and it makes me realize I still haven't seen him yet. The President. I've heard his voice, while Leon's on the phone with him. Leon Panetta, my boss – Chief of Staff.

She's proud of herself.

I haven't seen him, and I'm   curious.

HILLARY: Curious?

They share a look.

MONICA: Then the band starts playing...

THE SAXOPHONIST plays 'Hail to the Chief' and LINDA appears as BILL, BETTY as KIM YOUNG-SAM.

MONICA: …and there he is. Stepping out and waving. Greeting the President of South Korea, Kim Young-sam, whose name I wrote on my wrist in case it comes up in conversation.

BETTY: They're shaking hands…

LINDA: The President's arm around the man, squeezing his shoulder…

MONICA: And then they partake in the weird ritual: a twenty-one gun salute. Inspecting the military escort together – which feels more like North Korea to me.

LINDA: Then into the Blue Room…

BETTY: To sign the guest book…

LINDA: Then into the red room…

BETTY: For the exchange of gifts.

MONICA: Every arrival ceremony happens this way, in this exact order. And I guess I fixate on it because… I'm from *California*…so to me, all that rigid ritual is just so… *East Coast*.

CHELSEA: You're watching them exchange gifts

MONICA: He's smiling and waving, like I'd seen on TV so many times before, but now it's without the framing of the screen. I can look wherever I want. I can see his little flaws and specificities…

CHELSEA and BETTY examine LINDA AS BILL.

CHELSEA: A scuff mark on one of his shoes…

BETTY: A bead of sweat you can barely make out on his forehead…

MONICA: And that small bite of his lower lip – he really does that! – with a little head sway that says 'How great is this?' I can zoom in on these things. The access is jarring and performs the surprising function of…mammalizing the President.

CHELSEA: They remind you that his youth and energy and freshness are / actual traits

7

MONICA: Actual traits, emanating from an actual body.

BETTY: Not just product descriptions.

LINDA and BETTY circle the space.

MONICA: They're on their way to the State Dining Room, and about to pass by us.

CHELSEA: You and the other interns

MONICA: And I can zoom in on more of these traits:

BETTY: Oily glare off his nose...

CHELSEA: Wiry hair...

BETTY: Chunkier stomach than they show on TV...

MONICA: As he's fifty feet away...

CHELSEA: Twenty feet.

BETTY: Five feet.

MONICA: And in spite of all these flaws, or maybe because of them, I realize I'm *beaming.* Like some fucking fan girl.

CHELSEA: And then just for a moment...

BETTY: As he passes by...

MONICA: He sees me. Me and my beaming smile. And what happens then is...there's the slightest, tiniest departure from the ritual:

LINDA AS BILL's lips curl up into a grin.

He smiles back. For just a moment. And then they're passing by, through the doorway...

CHELSEA: Into the hallways of the White House.

MONICA: The White House...the place where I work now.

MONICA smiles at LINDA and BETTY passing by, then turns to HILLARY.

Is that how he told you it started?

HILLARY looks at her a beat, then...

HILLARY: I'm focused on narrative. Because soon the newspapers do run this ridiculous story, about an intern and the President, and that instantly legitimizes it. Ken Starr adds it to his investigation, new subpoenas as far as the eye can see... But fortunately, there's one upside of having gone through this so many times before: we know our first move.

CHELSEA steps forward as BILL.

HILLARY: Bill I need to get on the same page as you: Did you know this woman?

CHELSEA AS BILL: As much as any of 'em.

HILLARY: Were you ever alone with her?

CHELSEA AS BILL: She wanted help finding a job.

HILLARY: She was transferred to the Pentagon?

CHELSEA AS BILL: Staffers get transferred all the time.

HILLARY: Anything that would have given her an impression − ?

CHELSEA AS BILL: Impressionable.

HILLARY: Remember any physical...?

CHELSEA AS BILL: Maybe a touch, maybe a shoulder squeeze... You know how I am.

HILLARY nods.

LINDA: You put him on the interview circuit...

HILLARY: *NewsHour.*

CHELSEA AS BILL: I did not ask anyone to tell anything other than the truth. There is no improper relationship.

BETTY AS REPORTER: You had no sexual relationship with this young woman?

CHELSEA AS BILL: There is not a sexual relationship − that is accurate.

HILLARY: *Roll Call.*

LINDA AS REPORTER: You said earlier that you had no improper relationship / with this intern.

CHELSEA AS BILL: That's right −

LINDA AS REPORTER: But what exactly *was* the nature / of your –

CHELSEA AS BILL: But let me answer – it is *not* an improper relationship, and I know what the word means.

HILLARY: *All Things Considered*:

CHELSEA AS BILL: I have told people that I would cooperate in the investigation, and I expect to cooperate with it. I don't know any more about it than I've told you…

LINDA: And you start to pick up on something in his answers.

HILLARY: A sort of   timidity. I mark it as meekness in the face of fatigue, in the face of six years of non-stop accusations.

LINDA: But you know this situation calls for the opposite.

HILLARY goes to BETTY…

HILLARY: Hey Betty, is he free?

BETTY: Good evening, ma'am. He's still working with June and Begala on the speech, I think it'll –

HILLARY: Sure. How's it coming?

BETTY: He's only begged for Big Macs a couple times, that's pretty good for / him.

HILLARY: That's great. Focus is what he needs, and we'll keep this shit off his desk.

BETTY: This one's crazy, right? I had photographers following me to work.

HILLARY: Really? Did you tell Secret Service?

BETTY: I'm fine. How are you holding up?

HILLARY: I just thought we'd come out stronger. I saw the press he did yesterday – didn't you think he sounded weak?

BETTY: I didn't get to watch.

HILLARY: If we walk on eggshells like that, the other side gets to claim the narrative. It should be forceful.

BETTY: I guess it's an uncomfortable subject for a President, isn't it?

HILLARY: Well and the irony of it is the right knows they've gone too far this time. So if we could just flip it on them –

BETTY: Mm.

HILLARY: It would blow up in their face!

BETTY: I agree, ma'am.

> *Beat.*

Did you want me to pass on a message?

HILLARY: Sorry.

BETTY: No, it's / fine.

HILLARY: You must have a million things. Just tell him I'm in the residence, will you?

BETTY: Of course.

HILLARY: And Betty next time a photographer follows your car…just do what I do:

> *She flips her off and they laugh.*
>
> *HILLARY starts to go…then lingers…*

Did you know her? This girl?

BETTY: I met her a few times. She started   sometime around the shutdown.

> *HILLARY leaves, and the music shifts.*

MONICA: When the government shuts down, so does most of the West Wing. But not the interns! Unpaid means unfurloughed. Thanks, Newt.

CHELSEA AS INTERN: Okay here's one: which government service do you miss the least?

LINDA AS INTERN: IRS!

MONICA: DEA!

> *They laugh.*

MONICA: I've made some friends here. I'm a Washingtonian now. We're throwing a birthday party for one of Leon's assistants, Jennifer Palmieri.

LINDA: You step out to Leon's office

MONICA: And I'm dropping off some files when there's a little knock behind me.

BETTY appears behind her, as BILL.

BETTY AS BILL: Panetta?

LINDA: You don't even have to turn around.

CHELSEA: You know it's him.

MONICA: That voice. Again, same as on TV, but now without the filter of a speaker. I can hear how it wisps out into the air, the faint churning of specks of gravel in his throat. It's not even that it's attractive necessarily, just…familiar.

Beat.

By now there had been more smiles…

LINDA: Across hallways…

CHELSEA: Across the rope line…

MONICA: But now   in a room together.

BETTY AS BILL: Sorry, I was looking for Leon.

MONICA turns to face him.

You're one of the interns.

She nods, shy and nervous.

Why aren't you at the party?

MONICA: I bring the party with me.

HILLARY: You did *not* say that.

MONICA: Actually I don't remember. The truth is, I don't remember the words we exchanged here, and I bet he doesn't either, because it was one of those conversations where the words don't matter. They're just different-sized containers for electricity.

LINDA: But you make introductions…

MONICA: Monica.

BETTY AS BILL: *(Trying it out.)* Monica.

CHELSEA: You hear your name dusted with that gravel…

BETTY AS BILL: How do you like working in the White House?

MONICA: Workers get paid.

> *BETTY AS BILL chuckles.*

We're laughing and I'm overwhelmed by the momentousness of this, that the President has given even these few seconds – a fraction of a fraction of his running the world – over to me.

BETTY AS BILL: I've noticed you.

MONICA: I've noticed you.

BETTY AS BILL: Oh good, I'd have to fire some folks if you hadn't.

LINDA: And then as you finish laughing…

CHELSEA: There's a moment…

MONICA: A moment where this conversation will either end – and it would be clear what that means – or it will continue – and it would be clear what that means.

> *BETTY AS BILL bites her lip. Taps the doorway with her fingers.*

BETTY AS BILL: Well enjoy your little party in here. I guess I should go…

LINDA: He's saying he has to go

CHELSEA: but his feet take hesitant steps

LINDA: Signaling something

CHELSEA: Are you catching it?

LINDA: He needs it to be you.

MONICA: Oh do you um…need these files…?

> *She turns away from him.*

CHELSEA: The electricity's taken over

LINDA: Your heart is punching your chest

MONICA: And before I fully realize what I'm doing, I'm lifting up my jacket, just a few inches…just enough to show the lace pressing into my skin. And I'm sure we say something more, but I don't remember what, because again, it didn't matter. What mattered was that I had done this, that I had done this and that when I looked back at him walking out…he was still smiling.

She and BETTY smile at each other.

HILLARY: I have to remind myself you were twenty-two. It makes this all so much less…

LINDA: *(Offering.)* Consensual?

BETTY: No. Really?

LINDA: Yes really.

BETTY: You think a twenty-two-year-old can't decide / for herself –

LINDA: Under the influence of the most powerful man in the world?

CHELSEA: But she flashed him.

LINDA: Yeah and no one's ever been coerced into doing *that* before.

HILLARY: I was just going to say it makes it so much less original.

MONICA: You've never been seduced by power?

HILLARY: Not in the way you mean it.

MONICA: Oh come on, you / mean to –

HILLARY: Your turn's over.

She steps away.

HILLARY: Two days now 'til the State of the Union, and because of his weak answers, they're speculating about whether he'll address it. We're losing the narrative – so I come up with a one-two punch:

LINDA AS BILL: Should I just address it in the speech? Begala thinks –

HILLARY: Hell no, we can't grant it that kind of standing.

LINDA AS BILL: I thought you want me to punch back harder.

HILLARY: I do, but not in the State of the Union, Bill, it would / legitimize it.

LINDA AS BILL: Alright, but where then?

HILLARY thinks a beat.

HILLARY: Tomorrow's press conference.

LINDA AS BILL: No…

HILLARY: It's the only time between now and then / where –

LINDA AS BILL: It'll overshadow the childcare proposal, you've worked too / hard –

HILLARY: And if you don't do it, *everything* will get overshadowed. So let's just rip off the band-aid.

BETTY: And so he does:

CHELSEA: Everyone at school's talking about it.

HILLARY: Really?

CHELSEA: They're all doing impressions, 'I did not have sexual relations with that woman.'

HILLARY: Oh god, they do that in front of you?

CHELSEA: They hide it from me, but Matthew heard it. What was it like in the room?

HILLARY: It was really great, Chels, everyone applauded, there were all those families there for the rollout / and –

CHELSEA: Good.

HILLARY: I'm really proud of him.

CHELSEA: Me too. I hope it goes away.

Beat.

Just tell him to not say 'relations' next time.

HILLARY: What do you mean?

15

CHELSEA: 'Sexual relations?' I don't know, it's so weird...

HILLARY: Oh.

CHELSEA: Matthew asked me if that's how he normally talks, and I was like actually I've never heard anyone say that.

HILLARY: I think it's just the lawyers.

CHELSEA: Oh.

HILLARY: They get so specific about the language. I was prepping with them for the *Today* show...

CHELSEA: You're doing the *Today* show?

HILLARY: Yeah in the morning, I didn't tell you? Matt Lauer.

CHELSEA: But aren't they going to ask you about it?

HILLARY: Yes they will. He made his statement today, I'll do mine tomorrow, and when he gives the State of the Union it'll all be done with.

CHELSEA: Just don't say 'sexual relations'.

HILLARY: I can promise you that. So Matthew, huh? You're seeing him a lot?

CHELSEA: *(Instantly shy.)* He's just a friend.

HILLARY: Hm.

CHELSEA: I'm going. Tell Dad I hope he kills the speech.

HILLARY: He didn't call you today?

CHELSEA: He did. Just tell him again.

> *CHELSEA disappears.*
>
> *HILLARY thinks a beat as BETTY and LINDA appear around her. LINDA starts applying makeup on HILLARY, while BETTY, as MATT LAUER sits in a chair reviewing interview notecards.*
>
> *MONICA's circling the space.*

MONICA: I'm wandering the hallways of the furloughed West Wing and I am *reeling* from what I've just done. 'Cause what *have* I just done? Did I really just flash my Macy's thong at the President of the United States? And yeah he was smiling, but what if he was just being polite and actually thinks I'm a psychopath? What if the reason he left was to go tell Leon so they can blacklist me from ever setting foot in this place a –

CHELSEA AS BILL: Hey.

> *MONICA stops.*

Now I can't find Stephanopoulos! My whole senior staff seem to be missing. You haven't seen him, have you?

> *She shakes her head no.*

Where are you wandering to?

MONICA: I'm not sure.

CHELSEA AS BILL: Come here, I want to show you something…

MONICA: He opens a side door of the office and walks through it. Was he waiting for me? There's a light coming from the other side, and I follow him. Down a corridor, through his private dining room and into a little office – areas I'm not allowed to be.

CHELSEA AS BILL: This is my study.

MONICA: That wall, it's curved. Is that where the…?

CHELSEA AS BILL: Yep.

MONICA: Oh my god.

> *She stares at it.*

> *Blinding light shines on HILLARY, sitting opposite BETTY AS MATT LAUER.*

BETTY AS MATT LAUER: Mrs. Clinton, good morning.

HILLARY: Good morning, Matt.

BETTY AS MATT LAUER: This interview had been scheduled to talk about child care, but there's been one question on the minds of a lot of people in this country lately, and that is: What is the exact nature of the relationship between your husband and Monica Lewinsky? Has he described it to you?

HILLARY: We've talked at great length, and I think as this matter unfolds, the entire country will have more information. But right now we're in the middle of a rather vigorous feeding frenzy.

MONICA: I'm breathing in the air of forty-one presidents, as the forty-second one smiles down at me, ten feet from the Oval Office. That smile, with all of its warmth, and certainty, and sincerity...

CHELSEA AS BILL: So you always this much fun at work?

She shakes her head no.

Just me, huh?

She nods.

And why / is –

MONICA: I have a crush on you.

CHELSEA AS BILL smiles.

CHELSEA AS BILL: A crush?

MONICA: That sounded stupid.

CHELSEA AS BILL: No it didn't.

MONICA: Then why are you laughing?

CHELSEA AS BILL: 'Cause I'm trying to figure out how to ask if I can kiss you.

BETTY AS MATT LAUER: He's described in his words what this relationship was *not*. Has he described to you what it was?

HILLARY: *(To audience.)* I just want to remind everyone that this is Matt fucking Lauer asking me these questions.

Back to it.

Yes, Matt, and we'll find that out as time goes by. But I think the important thing now is to stand as firmly as I can and say that the President has denied these allegations on all counts, unequivocally.

MONICA: Mouths...lips...bra...it quickly becomes a blur.

HILLARY: Everybody says to me, how can you be so calm? And I guess I've just been through it so many times.

MONICA: His hand sliding down me…the same hand that thousands had shaken. Those fingers, that millions had seen pointed at them, now pointed at me…and with such intention…

HILLARY: I mean, Bill and I have been accused of everything, including murder, by some of the very same people who are behind these allegations.

MONICA: Then I find myself on my knees…my own fingers gliding over the fabric of his pants. My fingers, that no one had ever seen…

BETTY AS MATT LAUER: James Carville, who you know…

HILLARY: The Ragin' Cajun.

BETTY AS MATT LAUER: He has said this is war between the President and Kenneth Starr. You have said, I understand, that this is the last great battle, and that one side or the other is going down here.

HILLARY: Well, I don't know if I've been that dramatic. But I do believe that this is a battle. And the great story here for anybody willing to find it and write about it and explain it is this *vast right-wing conspiracy* that has been conspiring against my husband since the day he announced for president.

CHELSEA AS BILL: Stop!

MONICA: Why? I want you to finish.

CHELSEA AS BILL: Not yet. I need to know I can trust you.

> *CHELSEA AS BILL grips the desk to steady herself, out of breath.*

(Half-laughing.) Haven't, uh, had that in a while. What's your name again?

> *They smile at each other.*
>
> *The interview dissipates and HILLARY steps forward.*

HILLARY: Soon after this, at a state dinner we're hosting for the new young Prime Minister of the UK, I'm seated next to the Speaker of the House. And while we're eating our salmon, Newt leans over to me and whispers, 'These accusations against your husband are ludicrous. Terribly unfair. But don't worry – it won't go anywhere.' That was the moment I knew it worked. They went too far this time. His approval rating hits the highest of his presidency, sixty-six percent, and when he gets up in front of the nation and tells us the Union is strong, you know what? No one questions it.

> *THE SAXOPHONIST's music shifts...the improvisations become more bustling and intricate...*
>
> *An orchestrated, slick sequence unfolds:*
>
> *MONICA shows up at BETTY's desk with a plate of pizza.*

MONICA: Hi Ms. Currie, the President asked for some pizza from the party.

BETTY: You guys are having another party?

MONICA: *(With a smile.)* This damn shutdown. They're working us late a lot.

> *BETTY leans over to the door of the Oval.*

BETTY: Sir? The girl's here with the...pizza?

> *To MONICA.*

Go ahead...

> *She watches MONICA go into the office.*
>
> *Then just like that MONICA shows up at BETTY's desk again.*

MONICA: Ms. Currie, you work Sundays?

BETTY: Only when the President asks me to. How's your internship going, Ms. Lewinsky? Must be wrapping up soon...

MONICA: No, I'm a staffer now! Legislative Affairs.

BETTY: Oh. Guess that means we'll be seeing more of you. You must be excited?

MONICA: My friends took me out last night to celebrate – I tried my first cigar!

BETTY: Never liked the taste myself.

MONICA: Me either. But it felt cool!

BETTY: So did you...need something?

MONICA: Oh I just came in to get some weekend work done, and um...

> *She indicates papers in her hands, then something over BETTY's shoulder catches her eye.*

Oh hi Mr. President! You need me to what?

> *She smiles at BETTY.*

BETTY: *(Curious.)* Go ahead...

> *She watches MONICA walk in again.*

> *Then suddenly MONICA is at home, and her phone rings.*

MONICA: Hello?

BETTY: Ms. Lewinsky? This is Betty Currie from the White House.

MONICA: Oh hi Betty!

BETTY: I have the President for you.

> *The phone rings again and MONICA answers.*

MONICA: Hello?

BETTY: Hi Ms. Lewinsky, the President would like to know if you can come in Saturday afternoon for a meeting. Around three o'clock?

MONICA: I'll be there.

BETTY: Great.

> *Beat.*

So will I.

> *MONICA shows up in BETTY's office.*

MONICA: Hi Betty.

BETTY: Hi Ms. Lewinsky, he's in Colorado today, but –

MONICA: I know. I just wanted to leave something for him.

She hands BETTY a small gift box.

BETTY: Huh.

MONICA: What?

BETTY: He left this for you…

She hands MONICA a small gift box.

MONICA: What a coincidence. Thanks!

She steps away and opens it, pulling out a gold hat pin. She admires it.

Our little way of feeling closer than we're actually able to be. And we have grown close…except he still won't finish with me. When I try again he says:

LINDA AS BILL : Not yet. I can't get addicted to you.

MONICA: But the calls and the gifts keep coming, so I try not to let it bother me.

HILLARY: Didn't he –

She stops herself. MONICA looks over at her.

MONICA: What?

HILLARY: I don't mean to keep interrupting.

MONICA: And yet…

HILLARY: Well it is my play.

MONICA: Didn't he what?

HILLARY: Didn't he say the inverse as well? 'I can't get addicted to you' and 'I can't let *you* get addicted to *me.*'

MONICA: Oh this is where you start painting me as delusional…

HILLARY: No I just think if we're going to compare our versions, the details are important.

MONICA: Well the details are that he gave me a hat pin
and brooches and figurines, and I gave him shirts and
sunglasses and ties. And you know what? He wore them.

HILLARY: And what's the next detail?

A beat.

MONICA: They tell me I'm being transferred.

*Suddenly we're at BETTY's desk, and CHELSEA has
just walked up.*

BETTY: What's his name?

CHELSEA: Matthew Pierce. Isn't it a great name?

BETTY: Mm. /

CHELSEA: He's from outside of Houston, he's a junior – so
like really mature, but only a couple years older than me,
which is like a good balance, you know?

BETTY: What's his major?

CHELSEA: Religious studies.

BETTY: So mature.

CHELSEA: He's great. I like him a lot.

BETTY: Look how *old* you're getting, it's killing me.

CHELSEA: I'm not even in my twenties yet.

BETTY: Well I remember when you had those braces, / so…

CHELSEA: Oh my god those sucked ass.

BETTY: You *hated* 'em, I remember you fussing with that wax…

CHELSEA: The worst!

BETTY: But look at Miss Thang now. When do we get to meet
him?

CHELSEA: I'm going to ask Mom and Dad if he can come to
Martha's Vineyard with us in the summer.

BETTY: Aww. Now speaking of your dad, he's in a meeting
with the Joint Chiefs, but do you want / me to – ?

CHELSEA: No I came here to see you.

BETTY: Oh.

CHELSEA: Yeah I wanted to talk to you about...

She sighs.

BETTY: What is it?

CHELSEA: All those stories...about that girl. And his deposition or whatever that leaked today...

BETTY: Uh huh.

CHELSEA: They all mention you.

BETTY's demeanor shifts.

CHELSEA: Saying you delivered like letters and gifts, and took her down secret passageways or whatever...

BETTY: Chelsea, what you need to know –

CHELSEA: *(Suddenly upset.)* I just don't want you to be mad at us! I can't believe they're dragging you into this and and like *accusing*...

BETTY: Hey...

CHELSEA: When you've been working for my dad for so long, and –

BETTY: It's ok.

CHELSEA: I'm just really sorry, and I hope you're not resent / ful –

BETTY: Chelsea. Look at me. People who work in this building get accused of things. It comes with the rental agreement. Right? Now they're throwing more shit at your father than any president I've ever seen, but all of it goes away, doesn't it?

She nods.

BETTY: This will too. Because your dad never forgets who he cares about, and who he's fighting for.

CHELSEA: I'm just so sick of all the jokes. Like at first it was whatever, but all the freaking... 'I did not have sexual –' URRGGH it's so ANNOYING.

BETTY: I know it is. But the second you let that noise twist you up, they win.

HILLARY has entered.

HILLARY: She's right.

BETTY: *(To CHELSEA.)* So you know what a really smart person once told me to say?

BETTY flips her off and CHELSEA smiles.

CHELSEA: Ok.

HILLARY: *(To CHELSEA.)* I'll meet you up there?

CHELSEA: Yeah.

She walks off. HILLARY holds up a newspaper.

HILLARY: You saw they leaked his Paula Jones deposition?

BETTY: Yeah, wonder whose briefcase that fell out of.

HILLARY: Truly. What a nice final fuck-you before their case gets thrown out.

Beat.

I did get confused – When they spring the Lewinsky questions on him?

BETTY: Mm-hm.

HILLARY: He talks about – I guess Vernon was trying to help her find a job? And Bill says, 'I think Betty suggested he meet with her.' I just thought it was – You said you only met her a few times, right?

BETTY: *(Thinking.)* Um…

HILLARY: Sorry, I don't even know why I'm –

BETTY: No no no.

HILLARY: It'll be gone soon anyway.

BETTY: Yeah but let me… If I remember right, I thought Vernon could help because she wanted to come back here. She'd been transferred to the Pentagon, and I think she didn't care for it…

MONICA appears.

MONICA: The *Pentagon*?

LINDA AS BILL: Now just –

MONICA: Do I look like I'm trying to work / in the –

LINDA AS BILL: You know I want you here.

MONICA: Then tell them!

LINDA AS BILL: Look, a couple of people have noticed how close we've gotten, and they think it's   a little weird.

MONICA: Oh they think it's weird? Then they should transfer James Carville to the fucking Pentagon!

LINDA AS BILL: Look, it's just until re-election. They just want to make sure I'm focused during the campaign, and that there aren't any   surprises. Just until November.

MONICA: And then you'll bring me back?

LINDA AS BILL: Any job you want, I promise.

MONICA steps from the scene as it dissipates…

MONICA: So we're back to looks. Across rooms and rope lines. And only at the events I'm allowed to go to as a *Pentagon staffer*. I go to as many as I can…

HILLARY: 'I can't let you get addicted to me.'

MONICA: *(Ignoring her.)* And he calls me to make up for it.

The phone rings and she picks it up.

BETTY: Ms. Lewinsky? I have the President for you…

MONICA: Keeping what closeness we can as we count down to election day. Fantasizing about what job I might take; how we'll arrange each rendezvous.

CHELSEA: But it's not enough.

MONICA: Not enough to endure this place. The concrete walls, the beige uniforms, it all looks just like the prison it feels like. We don't even *do* wars anymore!

BETTY: You want to burst.

MONICA: I've been holding onto this secret for seven months, this insane secret, and it wants to explode right out of me.

CHELSEA: You're dying to tell someone.

MONICA: Anyone! My mom, my girlfriends – I want to shout it from the Washington Monument!

> *Beat.*

Then one day at work, I see the President's face smiling back at me. A big poster, decorating a woman's cubicle. I ask her about it, and she says she's not a fan of his, but keeps the poster up out of respect for the office. And we become friends...

> *LINDA appears.*

LINDA: *(Extending a hand.)* Hi, I'm Linda Tripp.

> *THE SAXOPHONIST's music shifts...*

MONICA: I tell her everything...

LINDA: You were transferred from the White House? Why?

MONICA: How we met, what we did...

LINDA: Holy shit.

MONICA: How we did it...

LINDA: Sorry, you did *what* with a cigar?

BETTY: It's an outlet you need...

CHELSEA: You only have these phone calls to cling to...

MONICA: Just enough to keep me afloat. To keep it fun. A great story that I'll have for the rest of my life, like old ladies who talk about their hotel romps with JFK. And now I have someone to share it with...

HILLARY: Are you really trying to tell us you saw it as a fun story?

MONICA: Are you really still asking me the same question over and over?

HILLARY: Maybe if you answered it /

MONICA: No I'd actually like to ask *you* something now.

HILLARY: I don't have to answer anything / from you.

MONICA: How did *you* see it? You'd read his Paula Jones deposition by now, you knew we'd at least been friendly. You're smart, you're anything but naive – so what did you think it was?

HILLARY: You need to understand the difference between naiveté and trust. Naiveté is an inability to see everything in front of you, trust is *choosing* not to. It's what partnerships are built on. So what did I think about it? I *didn't.* I was busy trying to get poor people child care.

MONICA: *(Challenging her.)* And when did that change?

HILLARY: *(Begrudgingly.)* When Chelsea kept complaining about the jokes.

CHELSEA: 'Sexual relations', ugh...

HILLARY: Because the wording *is* specific...and why should it have to be?

BETTY: It sends you back to his original interviews...

HILLARY looks through papers she's holding.

HILLARY: The ones I had found weak...and they were, but now I could see why:

CHELSEA AS BILL: 'There is no improper relationship.'

BETTY AS BILL: 'There is not a sexual relationship – that is accurate.'

LINDA AS BILL: 'It is not an improper relationship, and I know what the word means.'

HILLARY: *They're all present tense.*

Beat.

He didn't say 'There *was* no improper relationship', just... not one now. And the only time that's different is in the child care speech, when he says...

BETTY AS BILL: I did not –

HILLARY: Past tense.

BETTY AS BILL: – have sexual relations with that woman.

HILLARY: *Relations.* And Chelsea's right, that's not the way you'd say it if you didn't do *any* –

> *She stops short.*

LINDA: Or are you just falling into the trap?

HILLARY: Right, he's being precise because he *has* to be / precise.

CHELSEA: If he said 'I never touched her…'

BETTY: …and then a picture surfaced of grazing her shoulder –

HILLARY: That's what they're after, it's the only way they can win this.

BETTY: But you don't *want* precise.

HILLARY: No, I want guns blazing, I want fuck you and your investigation, Mr. Starr!

CHELSEA: But then why isn't *he* being guns / blazing?

HILLARY: Right – No because he *needs* to be careful, of course he does.

CHELSEA: Doesn't he?

BETTY: You question this as you sit on the Truman Balcony, papers spread out in front of / you.

HILLARY: There *is* no improper relationship. No. There is *no* improper relationship. No. There is no *improper* relationship. I'm reading too much into this, I'm being… I'm being…

LINDA: *(Taunting.)* Vast right-wing conspiracy…

HILLARY: 'Cause if there was something to tell he would tell me, *we've done this before!*

> *She slams the papers down.*

HILLARY: I choose *trust.* This is the last battle, I know it is.

> *Beat.*

It *is.*

Beat.

Isn't it?

> *Confetti falls – or maybe the others throw it into the air – as THE SAXOPHONIST plays celebratory music.*

CHELSEA: Four more years!

CHELSEA/BETTY: Four more years! Four more years!

> *MONICA has appeared.*

MONICA: Finally... Election night. I see Leon there on the TV, beaming, having turned this ship around. And I worked for him! I was part of it!

BETTY: You're deciding what you should say when he calls...

MONICA: Congratulations, Mr. President. Congrats, Bill. Can't wait to welcome you back to the White House. A proper welcome.

CHELSEA: You're too excited again...

BETTY: You have to share it with someone...

> *MONICA picks up her phone.*

LINDA: Can't believe people want four more years of that turd.

MONICA: Linda!

LINDA: You know I'm a Bush gal, I still think about what his second term could have been like. Maybe Jeb'll run in 2000...

MONICA: Who's Jeb? /

LINDA: These Clintons, they're just always surrounding themselves with the worst kinds of people – except you, sweetie.

MONICA: He's really just trying to do good.

LINDA: Oh come on...

MONICA: I know first-hand, ok? And I wouldn't work for an administration I didn't believe in.

LINDA: So you're really going to leave me and go back there?

MONICA: As soon as humanly possible.

LINDA: Monica… You're being careful, right?

MONICA: Of course I am. You're the only one who knows.

LINDA: I know, I just… I don't give a rat's ass about them, but I adore you, and… Just don't forget their power. I really think we don't know what they're capable of.

MONICA: You sound like Newt.

> *A little laugh.*

Well I just wanted to say hi. I should get off in case he calls.

LINDA: *(Annoyed.)* When are you going to get call waiting? It's almost the millennium.

MONICA: Byyyyyy/yyyye.

LINDA: Byyyye.

> *LINDA leaves.*

CHELSEA: Three AM…

BETTY: Four AM…

MONICA: But it's an hour earlier in Little Rock. He must have so many parties to go to…

BETTY: You fall asleep next to the phone…

CHELSEA: Dutifully waiting…

BETTY: Patiently loyal…

CHELSEA: Until the next morning –

> *The phone rings. MONICA awakes and answers it.*

MONICA: Hello?!

LINDA: Has he called yet?

MONICA: Ugh.

> *She hangs up.*

BETTY: Then November goes by…

CHELSEA: December…

BETTY: Inauguration…

MONICA: It takes three months. Three months of silence until finally:

CHELSEA AS BILL: Hey sugar.

MONICA: Bill. It's been so long…

CHELSEA AS BILL: It's been so busy.

MONICA: Months? Too busy to call for months?

CHELSEA AS BILL: What's wrong?

MONICA: What's wrong? I'm still at the Pentagon. You were going to bring me back, remember?

CHELSEA AS BILL: Of course we're / gonna –

MONICA: But when? I / want to –

CHELSEA AS BILL: We'll talk about it this week, I promise. But I don't want to talk about that tonight. Tonight… It's been so long…

MONICA: I miss being there.

CHELSEA AS BILL: I do too.

MONICA: What do you miss?

CHELSEA AS BILL: Your smile. And I miss the sneakin' around of it, don't you?

MONICA: I want you to fuck me.

LINDA: He says

CHELSEA AS BILL: You know we can't do that.

MONICA: But I want it, why can't we?

CHELSEA AS BILL: Too risky, baby. Consequences are too big.

MONICA: They're not already?

CHELSEA AS BILL: Maybe I shouldn't be calling…

MONICA: No no I'm glad you're calling. I want to see you. It's been almost a *year*. Can I see you?

LINDA: He breathes heavily.

BETTY: He tells you it has to be done carefully.

CHELSEA AS BILL: We invite guests in to watch the weekly radio address. I'll have Betty arrange it.

MONICA: I'll be there.

> *MONICA hangs up the phone.*

> *THE SAXOPHONIST's music shifts as HILLARY and MONICA each begin undressing.*

HILLARY: A woman can be perceived as one of two things: an object of sex, or an object of power.

MONICA: Sometimes the two can co-exist.

HILLARY: Rarely. Mostly it's one or the other.

> *They finish undressing, HILLARY revealing a simple nightgown underneath, and MONICA a slip.*

> *The other three are around them.*

I feel guilty that night as I lie next to him.

MONICA: I feel anxious as I think about what gift I should bring him.

HILLARY: Guilty for my doubts.

MONICA: 'Cause what do you get the man who has nukes?

> *HILLARY lies down.*

HILLARY: So I sidle up behind him. I rest my face on his shoulder blade. I want to remind him I'm more than just his political partner…that power isn't my only object; isn't my object at all, really. That it's always been rooted in love…

MONICA: A message in *The Washington Post*:

'To Handsome,

With love's light wings did
I o'er perch these walls
For stony limits cannot hold love out,
And what love can do that dares love attempt.
– Romeo and Juliet, Act Two Scene Two
Happy Valentines Day
M'

LINDA: She really did that, by the way.

HILLARY: I am his devotion. He is my tenderness. We're the ones who trust each other...even when no one else will...

> *She falls asleep.*

MONICA: And then I think...why not a gift for myself too?

> *A navy blue dress from The Gap appears.*
>
> *MONICA gazes at it. Picks it up.*
>
> *She slips it on, with care. This can take a while.*
>
> *And then MONICA is standing before us in the blue dress. The MONICA we remember.*
>
> *She walks into the Oval Office, and locks eyes with CHELSEA, BETTY and LINDA (all AS BILL).*

LINDA AS BILL: Monica.

CHELSEA AS BILL: I hope you know how sorry I am that / it's taken –

MONICA: Kiss me.

BETTY AS BILL: Easy tiger.

> *She smiles at MONICA.*

LINDA AS BILL: I saw your sweet, sweet message

CHELSEA AS BILL: In the *Post*

BETTY AS BILL: Just lovely

LINDA AS BILL: So I wanted to give you somethin' in return.

> *They produce a book, and hand it to MONICA.*
>
> *She looks at it.*

MONICA: *Leaves of Grass.*

BETTY AS BILL: Walt Whitman.

CHELSEA AS BILL: Most beautiful thing I ever read.

LINDA AS BILL: I thought that   you might be that special kind of person who could appreciate it.

MONICA: *(Reading.)* 'That you are here – that life exists, and identity; That the powerful play goes on, and you will contribute a verse.'

(Deeply appreciative.) Thank you.

> *She smiles, touched, and sets the book down.*

MONICA: Then we're kissing, but it's different this time. He's unbuttoning my new dress, I'm unbuttoning him… but there's something new about it. Something that's blossomed in the time we've been apart.

> *The three of them freeze.*

BETTY AS BILL: Did you hear that?

LINDA AS BILL: I think there's someone in the office.

MONICA: It's ok. Let's go into the bathroom.

> *They move near where HILLARY is sleeping.*

And we do, and I return to my knees and that's different too now. I'm still not sure what it is, but this time I'm determined to show him I *am* that special kind of person.

BETTY AS BILL: Stop.

MONICA: I don't want to stop.

CHELSEA AS BILL: We can't –

MONICA: Why?

BETTY AS BILL: You know it's too risky.

MONICA: I care about you so much now. And I want to make you finish.

LINDA AS BILL: Fuck.

MONICA: When you don't…it's not complete. And I know it's not complete for you either.

> *Beat.*

It's okay. You can trust me.

> *LINDA, BETTY and CHELSEA bite their lips.*

MONICA: And then we're closer than ever before. After all these months, we've reunited into something so much deeper than I ever imagined…something I realize in that moment I've never felt before: *love.*

> *LINDA, BETTY and CHELSEA shift their attention. They look down on HILLARY sleeping.*

LINDA AS BILL: Hillary.

CHELSEA AS BILL: Hillary.

BETTY AS BILL: Honey, wake up.

> *She opens her eyes. Sees them and smiles.*

HILLARY: Hey baby. How'd you sleep?

BETTY AS BILL: Oh Hillary. That story…

CHELSEA AS BILL: It's true.

LINDA AS BILL: All of it.

BETTY AS BILL: And she's handed over this   dress

LINDA AS BILL: this blue dress

CHELSEA AS BILL: with evidence.

LINDA AS BILL: I have to tell the nation tonight.

> *She sits there frozen.*
>
> *A long, terrible silence.*

BETTY AS BILL: I'm so / sorry.

HILLARY: Shh.

> *She sees 'Leaves of Grass' lying there next to her. She picks it up. Looks at it.*
>
> *She abruptly cocks her arm like she's going to throw it at them. Arm shaking. Body shaking.*
>
> *But then she lowers her arm to her side.*

INTERMISSION.

Article Two: Obstruction of Justice

Lights come up on MONICA, in new clothes, looking at the blue dress in her hands.

LINDA is watching her.

LINDA looks around and sees she has the space to herself. She looks out at us.

LINDA: This has all been fine. But I think it'd be healthy
for you to hear from more than just liberal women.
Does anyone object? Because all this…*theater*…it's just
window-dressing. The spectacle of these events has always
overshadowed the *substance*. Here are the objective,
knowable facts of what actually happened: a politician had
a swarm of affairs while governor and President, and all of
them included some measure of predation. He lied about
one affair while being deposed about another. And that lie
happened to get caught, because…

> *Something catches MONICA's eye, near the hip of the
> dress. A small stain.*
>
> *She examines it.*

…for the first time in his long career, there was something
more than he-said-she-said. There was *evidence*.

> *MONICA looks out at us.*

MONICA: Unexpected White House souvenir.

> *Rubbing it.*

Out, damned spot.

LINDA: Ugh, more theater. You're not Shakespearean, Monica!
Let me show you the difference between a liberal woman
and a conservative woman: The bleeding heart, blinded by
its untenable passions and fantastical notions of goodness,
would allow without a second thought the erasure of this
evidence:

MONICA: I guess I'll get it dry-cleaned.

37

LINDA: Not so the conservative woman. Her shrewdness
– what *you* might call her selfishness, but is really her
individualism, predicated on expecting goodness from *no
one* – leads her to a different conclusion:

She turns to MONICA.

Maybe don't.

MONICA: What?

LINDA: Maybe   hold onto it.

MONICA: Why?

LINDA: Just in case.

MONICA: In case of what?

CHELSEA and BETTY have appeared.

CHELSEA: You tell her

LINDA: I know how you feel about him today. And I know
why you feel the way you do. But you have a very long life
ahead of you.

MONICA: Uh huh.

LINDA: And I would rather you have that in your possession if
you need it, years from now. That's all.

MONICA: Years from now? You think I can hold onto a dress
with come on it for / ten or –

LINDA: Hey listen, my cousin is a genetic whatchamacalit,
and he said that on a rape victim now, if she's preserved a
pinprick size of crusted semen…

MONICA: Rape / victim?

LINDA: She can, ten, twenty years out, if she takes a wet Q-Tip
to it, it's still usable.

MONICA: Okay…?

LINDA: And look I'm just saying what I'd tell my own
daughter: god-willing, you'll never need it. But…

BETTY: You tell her

LINDA: ...just in case things don't go the way you hope they will...it could be your insurance policy. Just an insurance policy. Because I never, ever want to read about you going off the deep end because someone calls you a crazy liar / and

MONICA: Okay.

LINDA: you're left with no way to prove what actually –

MONICA: Okay! I'll think about it.

LINDA looks back out at us.

LINDA: See, if you look past all the scenery and the subterfuge here...this is just another story of mammalian urges. So treat it as such. Read Ayn Rand: 'The greatest sensation of existence: not to trust but to *know*.' So the woman who gets ahead here is the woman who trusts least.

She turns back to MONICA.

MONICA: Thank you.

LINDA: Of course.

MONICA: There's no one else I can...

LINDA: *(Smiling.)* I know.

HILLARY has appeared elsewhere, watching them.

HILLARY: Well why don't we just let *everyone* make this play about themselves!

To audience member.

How about you, sir, would you like your perspective considered?

LINDA: I'm just trying to provide some objectivity.

HILLARY: I see. An unbiased account.

LINDA: Yes.

HILLARY: But I thought the one who gets ahead most is the one who trusts least. So shouldn't we not trust anyone's account...including yours?

They all think a beat.

CHELSEA: It is kind of circular logic.

LINDA: No it's not, accepting facts doesn't / require any –

BETTY: Oh your version gets to be called facts.

LINDA: My version is the fucking / facts.

MONICA: Excuse me! Can we um…?

> *She indicates she'd like to get back to the scene.*

> *LINDA clears her throat, gets back to their phone call:*

LINDA: So you're seeing each other in person again?

> *MONICA holds up a paper that's just appeared.*

MONICA: And about to be moving back in.

> *MONICA crosses to BETTY's desk and hands her the paper.*

BETTY: You made a list.

MONICA: He said any White House job I'm interested in. These are the dream ones.

BETTY: I see.

MONICA: I haven't seen you in so long, Betty, how are you?

BETTY: *(Gritted smile.)* Working hard, Ms. Lewinsky.

> *She looks over the list.*

MONICA: You know…you can call me Monica. After all this time.

> *Beat.*

And just so you know… No one sees us here.

> *BETTY looks up at her.*

And as long as no one sees us…nothing has to have / happened –

BETTY: Stop. Please stop.

> *BETTY sets the paper down.*

Do you know how many Democratic presidents I've seen in my lifetime?

> *She shakes her head no.*

BETTY: Four. Mr. Kennedy was shot, Mr. Johnson couldn't run for re-election because of Vietnam, and Mr. Carter, well Mr. Carter was beat out by that *actor*. That's when I got involved: I worked for Mr. Mondale, who lost; then I worked for Mr. Dukakis, who lost; and then I went to work for the governor of Arkansas, who no one had ever heard of, let alone thought could be President. And yet look at us now, about to do something the Democrats haven't done in half a century: finish a second term.

> *Beat.*

So I will look over this list of your   'dream jobs', but I just want you to appreciate how much hard work it's taken to get us all here. You understand...Ms. Lewinsky?

> *A harsh silence – as HILLARY enters.*

HILLARY: Hey Betty, does he have a sec?

> *BETTY and MONICA are both startled.*

BETTY: Mrs. Clinton... I thought you were in New Hampshire today...

HILLARY: Got pushed to this afternoon. I want to show him this study before I go, I think there's an opening to pursue child care.

BETTY: I'll um   let him know you're here.

> *BETTY glances at MONICA, then goes into the office.*
>
> *HILLARY notices MONICA staring at her, smiles back politely.*

HILLARY: Hello.

MONICA: *(Mouthing the word.)* Hi.

> *BETTY returns.*

BETTY: Go ahead, ma'am.

HILLARY: Thanks.

> *HILLARY glances at MONICA once more – a slight curiosity piqued – then leaves.*
>
> *As the scene dissipates around her, HILLARY looks out to us...*

HILLARY: As I lie in our bed, sifting through the rubble of the bomb he's just dropped on me, memories like that one begin visiting me. Thousands of little memories, now imbued with entirely new meaning.

CHELSEA: You stay in the residence for hours.

HILLARY: For the first time since we've lived in this house, I just sit.

CHELSEA: Feeling the current of his confession.

LINDA: Criss-crossing the circuitry of those offices below you.

HILLARY: I know he'll be back soon. There's something he forgot to ask, something that needs to be sheepishly, pathetically requested...

BETTY: And your answer is ready:

HILLARY: No. Do it however you want: press conference, Oval address, Barbara Walters, I don't care, but no, I will not be standing by your side. Oh, and before you tell the nation? You better tell your daughter first.

LINDA: Every ounce of your body screaming to unleash

BETTY: Screaming to do something

HILLARY: I'm not sure yet what

BETTY: But you have to make it to tomorrow

CHELSEA: To Martha's Vineyard

BETTY: Get through today and tomorrow you can uncork

LINDA: Tomorrow you can figure it all out

HILLARY: He's down there giving his revised testimony to the grand jury, and I'm left to picture it. To picture his smug face as he weaves in and out of perjury traps, and dissections of what the word 'is' is. I hope they give him the graphic questions, the really intimate questions – no *relations*, no more euphemisms – and I hope he's made to suffer as surely I am only beginning to.

MONICA: Oh, and *I'm* Shakespearean?

HILLARY: *Quiet.*

MONICA: This is some *actual* Lady Macbeth shit.

HILLARY: Well maybe at some point you start playing the part people cast you in. Maybe at some point you have to bend to their will so you don't break in half.

LINDA: Except...

HILLARY: Except what?

LINDA: You'd already been through this before. When he was governor. Hadn't you?

BETTY: Gennifer Flowers.

LINDA: So do you really expect us to believe   you were surprised?

BETTY: I always assumed they had an understanding.

CHELSEA: Based on what?

HILLARY: You could consider for a second, if I'd known it was true, whether I would have gone on national television and said 'vast right-wing conspiracy'. No past experience could have prepared me for this exact brand of public shame, and none of you will ever know it.

MONICA: I know something of it.

HILLARY: You know the shame engendered by your own sins – fair enough and so does he – but that's not the same as having defended your partner, in front of a nation, having *gloated* at your opposition, laughed at the *preposterousness* of their allegations, only to –

> *Stops herself.*

The surprise was that he would let me experience that.

CHELSEA: You finally leave the room.

HILLARY: He's about to tell Senior Staff, and I feel an obligation to show my face, because they're the only ones who are about to feel something similar:

> *BETTY appears, along with CHELSEA and LINDA as senior staff.*

LINDA AS STAFFER: Sir, I think it should be a primetime address, and I think you need to apologize.

CHELSEA AS STAFFER: No, that's giving them too much / credit.

LINDA AS STAFFER: If he doesn't then that becomes the whole story.

HILLARY: My ears are still ringing. So I just look at all of them. Betrayed. Shocked.

> *Glancing at BETTY.*

Some less than others…

> *BETTY averts.*

CHELSEA AS STAFFER: If he apologizes, we can't call out the investigation for –

LINDA AS STAFFER: We can do both if he just first / says he's *sorry.*

CHELSEA AS STAFFER: No one will take it seriously, this has to be / about an invasion –

LINDA AS STAFFER: It's about avoiding *impeachment* now, / are you crazy?

CHELSEA AS STAFFER: No it's – It is not, it's about an invasion into personal bullshit!

HILLARY: Enough! Let him write the damn thing himself.

> *CHELSEA and LINDA leave.*

> *BETTY lingers…*

BETTY: Ma'am, I don't know what to say.

HILLARY: Go back to your fucking desk.

> *BETTY lingers a beat, then goes, just as a phone rings.*

BETTY: Ms. Lewinksy, the President would like to arrange a meeting.

> *MONICA appears at her desk.*

MONICA: What job did they pick? Do you know?

BETTY: *(Pointing to the office.)* The President will see you now.

MONICA walks in, and CHELSEA AS BILL appears.

CHELSEA AS BILL: We can't do this anymore.

MONICA's hit in the gut.

Quite a few beats.

I'm sorry. We let it go too far…

MONICA: Too far? No one knows…

LINDA: But he tells you about other affairs, from early in his marriage.

CHELSEA AS BILL: When I became President, I put an end to all that. Then I had to go and meet you…

Beat.

But I very much want to be your friend.

MONICA: My friend? Is this fucking high school?

LINDA: You're standing there with the gifts you brought him

BETTY: Banana Republic shirt and a puzzle

LINDA: You're trembling

CHELSEA AS BILL: I told you we can't get addicted to each other.

MONICA: I'm not addicted if I want to see you, if I want to –

CHELSEA AS BILL: I'm not saying that. But we're doing more here than we said we would, and…

MONICA: And what?

CHELSEA AS BILL: We just can't.

She goes to him.

MONICA: You know this is crazy. Come on –

He rebuffs her.

She stands there, chastened.

Then maybe I'll just…go to New York   and

CHELSEA AS BILL: If that's what you want, we'll help. We'll take care of you.

LINDA: Already transitioning his language

BETTY: Words meant to mollify

MONICA: I want to be back *here*, like you promised.

CHELSEA AS BILL: We can do that too. I'll have Betty talk to Vernon.

MONICA: You really want this?

CHELSEA AS BILL: It's how it has to be.

The scene dissipates.

LINDA: You place calls...

MONICA: But now I can't get through.

BETTY: You try letters...

MONICA: 'Dear Handsome, I'd really like to discuss my situation with you...'

CHELSEA: Asking if you can just talk

MONICA: But it becomes clear we have very different ideas of friendship.

BETTY: Or maybe you're not that special kind of person after all...

MONICA: So I go back to the Pentagon, ready to start a war of my own:

LINDA and MONICA on a phone call.

LINDA: Slow down.

MONICA: They won't even let him *talk* to me.

LINDA: We knew something like this would happen.

MONICA: I know but –

LINDA: These people are completely –

MONICA: You know I don't like when you call them that!

LINDA: Look at you, you're still defending them!

MONICA: Defending *him*! Because they're making him do this, I / know they are!

LINDA: Monica list – Why don't you do what you were saying and go to New York? You could get away from all this.

MONICA: But they promised they'd bring me back and I want them to! I want to work there again!

LINDA: Listen –

MONICA: If I go back, we can be together, I know it. I could hear it in his voice. But now they've convinced him to fuck me over and I feel completely helpless and disposable, like / I'm some –

LINDA: *(Exploding.)* Listen to yourself! Monica. Listen to yourself. Who has the upper hand here?

> *Beat.*

Who has the upper hand here?

> *Somewhere near them, the blue dress is illuminated or appears.*

HILLARY: Object of sex, or object of power.

> *MONICA goes to it and takes it in her arms.*

I am briefly neither, as the President delivers an address about our marriage to seventy million people:

BETTY AS BILL: Indeed I did have a relationship with Ms. Lewinsky that was not appropriate.

HILLARY: Maybe it's masochistic to watch, but I'm curious what he'll say…

BETTY AS BILL: In fact, it was wrong.

HILLARY: I'm curious because there's this little part of me, whatever little part isn't numb from the shock of the blast, that's been appraising him throughout the day. Ever since he told me. What it's appraising, I'm not yet sure…

CHELSEA: But you can't uncork yet

LINDA: Not until tomorrow

> *MONICA looks up from the dress.*

MONICA: 'Dear *Sir,* My parents were under the impression I'd be returning to the White House after the election. So if I'm not, I'll need to explain to them exactly *why* that isn't happening…'

Phone rings.

BETTY: Ms. Lewinsky? The President would like to see you.

MONICA is in the office with CHELSEA AS BILL, who's irate.

CHELSEA AS BILL: What are you thinkin' sending something like that to the White House?!

MONICA: I needed to get / your –

CHELSEA AS BILL: Don't you know it's illegal to threaten the President of the / United States!

MONICA: YOU SAID YOU WANTED TO BE FRIENDS AND YOU CAN'T EVEN GIVE ME THAT!

CHELSEA AS BILL: I'm doing the best I can!

MONICA: I call Betty and she won't tell me where you are, I ask Vernon about the job and he never gets / back to me.

CHELSEA AS BILL: They're working on the job.

MONICA: I don't get it, you're the President, just tell them to hire me and they'll hire me. Don't you want me back here?

CHELSEA AS BILL: Of course I do!

MONICA: Then why –

CHELSEA AS BILL: BECAUSE I – !

They're quiet a beat.

MONICA: It's her, isn't it. You're afraid to bring me back because of her.

CHELSEA AS BILL lets out a big sigh.

CHELSEA AS BILL: It's a lot of things. You've seen how hard they're comin' after me – now I gotta testify about this Paula Jones bullshit? The President, being deposed!

MONICA: We can navigate that. I think we make a great team…don't you?

> *She touches his arm. Something shifts in CHELSEA AS BILL's look.*

CHELSEA AS BILL: Listen… There's a good chance I'll be alone in a few years. Once I'm out of office. You understand?

LINDA: You nod

BETTY: You think you understand

CHELSEA AS BILL: Let's play this smart. Let's wait. And if I'm not too old a man for you by then…

> *They share a smile.*

…then we could be together.

> *HILLARY lets out a big exhale.*

HILLARY: He always knew how to inspire hope.

> *MONICA turns to HILLARY.*

MONICA: If I'll never understand your shame, you'll never know my lack of agency.

HILLARY: You had agency at crucial moments. One very crucial moment in particular, when you decided to *wade into something.*

MONICA: I was twenty-two, it shouldn't have been so easy!

HILLARY: I agree!

> *They break away from each other…*

MONICA: I pack for New York…

HILLARY: I pack for Martha's Vineyard…

MONICA: I can start over there. I can learn to wait.

HILLARY: Washington's exploding, and impeachment's in the air.

> *HILLARY grabs CHELSEA's arm and they circle the stage holding hands…*

CHELSEA: We're crossing the South Lawn

BETTY: Towards the army of cameras on your way to the helicopter

CHELSEA: The First Family's departure ceremony

BETTY: Chelsea between you, holding each of your hands like tape on a pair of broken glasses

> *Flashbulbs blind them.*

> *MONICA's folding the blue dress.*

LINDA: You're ready to leave this place, ready to wrap your secret in a box

MONICA: Maybe I'm not a Washingtonian after all.

HILLARY: We lift into the air and I see that house below us shrink in size. And as it gets smaller and smaller, as we leave this place, that little part of me, the one that's been watching him in appraisal…

BETTY: It tugs at you.

CHELSEA: Ready to deliver a verdict.

HILLARY: And it tells me I should leave him too.

> *A phone rings.*

MONICA: Hello?

BETTY: Ms. Lewinsky, it's Betty Currie from the White House.

MONICA: It's okay, Betty. I don't want a job there anymore.

BETTY: That's not why I'm calling. I'm going to put you on with the White House counsel, okay?

MONICA: Why?

BETTY: Just give me a moment.

MONICA: *(Pleading.)* Betty…?

BETTY: *(A beat.)* You've been added as a character witness in the Paula Jones lawsuit. And a subpoena is coming.

> *Music swells as the lights go dark.*

> *When the music ends, lights come up to reveal BETTY alone.*

> *She smiles at us.*

BETTY: There's a lot being said here by people who don't have decades of experience to back it up. So how about an aside from someone who's earned her time here?

Saxophonist starts to play until...

Just a moment.

Out.

I know this is the part in a play where fatigue can set in, so I'll keep it brief.

Beat.

Something I learned to value early in my career is loyalty. If the boss is staying past five, *you don't ask* if you're staying past five. If he doesn't go out to lunch, you eat yours quietly at your desk. And if he brings someone to his office via the back hallway, when that person returns, *you* take them via the back hallway.
This loyalty is predicated on mutual trust: I will not ask why I'm taking them via the back hallway, because he will ensure it is never necessary for me to know.
Now: was that trust violated?

The others have appeared.

CHELSEA: January 1998...

LINDA AS BILL leans against the desk and folds her arms.

LINDA AS BILL: Betty, I gave my deposition for the Paula Jones bullshit yesterday, and they asked me about our, uh, frequent visitor.

BETTY: Oh.

LINDA AS BILL: So you may be hearing about it in the news soon. Now I imagine there are several things you may want to know.

BETTY: Yes sir?

LINDA AS BILL: For instance: were we ever alone together? Well if you think about it, this door here was always cracked open, wasn't it? And the door on the other side there, the one to my study, well I never close that one, do I?

BETTY: No sir.

LINDA AS BILL: And whenever she was here…it would be fair to say that you were here too, isn't that right?

BETTY: I don't know, sir.

LINDA AS BILL: Fair enough, because how would you know about the times you weren't here. Well the White House logs seem to tell that story, and they're accurately kept, aren't they?

BETTY: That's true, sir, they are.

LINDA AS BILL: So assuming you were here whenever she was here, and with those doors always being open…

BETTY: Yes sir, I see your meaning.

LINDA AS BILL: And what is my meaning, Betty?

BETTY: You were never alone with her.

LINDA AS BILL nods, and stands from the desk.

LINDA AS BILL: Did you notice her coming by, wanting to see me a lot?

BETTY: Yes sir.

LINDA AS BILL: Okay good, so we both noticed that *she* was coming onto *me.*

BETTY: I never saw you touch her, sir.

LINDA AS BILL nods. Bites her lip.

HILLARY: Some might see your willingness to turn a blind eye as enabling.

BETTY: And what do they see in your blind eye?

HILLARY: Denial is different than deniability, Betty, I'd have thought you'd know that by now.

CHELSEA: Others might point to his persuasion and see you as one of his victims.

LINDA: Bingo.

BETTY: Yes they might, but I am neither, and both miss the point. Loyalty means intrinsic commitment as a matter of *identity*. As a lifelong Democrat, for one – and you've heard my case on that front – but also… Consider a moment that among this man's many nicknames, the one bestowed upon him by Toni Morrison was? America's First Black President. Now her meaning's been misconstrued, she was talking about fast food and saxophones and how in these scandals he was, like a black man on the street, presumed guilty. But the mere *existence* of that nickname should illuminate how little hope there was of seeing an *actual* black president in our lifetime. This pasty lawyer from Arkansas would have to do; and so he would *succeed*. And you better believe I would make every effort to *ensure* he succeeds. But   how he goes about succeeding? Not something I enable, nor something by which I'm victimized. As any good secretary will tell you: that's above my pay grade.

> *She offers a sly smile.*

> *MONICA has begun gathering the gifts around the stage and putting them into a cardboard box.*

MONICA: And what about travelling to staffers' apartments? Is that above your pay grade?

> *They glare at each other a beat; then BETTY steps in to MONICA's apartment.*

> *MONICA holds up the box.*

BETTY: That's all of them?

> *MONICA picks up 'Leaves of Grass' and looks at it.*

Leaves of Grass?

MONICA: He gave it to me when I came in for the radio taping. The last time we…

> *BETTY waits.*

> *MONICA places it in the box with the others, and hands it over to BETTY.*

BETTY: I like your apartment. Who knew you lived at the Watergate?

> *MONICA starts to cry.*

BETTY: Don't do that.

MONICA: I don't have a lawyer, I don't / know how to answer –

BETTY: They're getting you a lawyer.

MONICA: I don't know if I should *trust* their lawyer – I don't want to get him in trouble, you know that, but I can't *lie*, Betty!

BETTY: No one is asking / you to lie.

MONICA: But what do I say when / they –

BETTY: If they had anything on you, you'd know by now. They're calling in any women who've ever talked with the President.

MONICA: Where are you taking those?

BETTY: We're going to hold onto them for a little while.

MONICA: Where, at the White House?

> *On her look.*

Your apartment?

BETTY: Just until things blow over.

MONICA: But his gifts are mentioned in the subpoena, won't I get in trouble / if I –

BETTY: *(Throwing the box down.)* Listen to me you little bitch. This political dilettante costume you've had on loan is far past overdue. The ball is *over*. I have already warned you, you will not be the piece that makes this tower crumble, and this will be the last time we discuss it.

> *Beat.*

Now pick up that fucking box, and hand it to me, and understand that it means you never *got* any gifts from the President.

> *MONICA collects herself. She picks up the box.*
>
> *She hands it to BETTY.*

BETTY: Thank you. Now. You will call the lawyer. He will tell you that to avoid appearing for a deposition, you may submit a written affidavit. Do you know what that is?

MONICA: Y/es.

BETTY: Good. And you know what to say in it.

> *MONICA nods.*
>
> *BETTY touches her shoulder and MONICA looks up at her. BETTY smiles.*

Then you'll be fine.

> *BETTY leaves with the box.*
>
> *MONICA stands there, on what is now a totally empty stage.*
>
> *Beach sounds fill the space – tranquil, soft – as HILLARY appears, sitting on a porch.*

HILLARY: There are those lame jokes about women making their men sleep on couches. 'In the dog house.' But I don't have to say anything.

LINDA: You're on the porch, watching him.

CHELSEA: Jogging on the beach with his dog.

HILLARY: I'm watching him as I make my plans to leave him.

LINDA: Your first impulse?

HILLARY: Immediate departure. Empty box seat at the next State of the Union, dancing by himself at state dinners. Who even *knows* what disarray the floral arrangements would fall to without the First Lady there?

CHELSEA: But...

HILLARY: That would kill any chance he has left at policy. Including child care. So, okay, worth the small wait.

BETTY: The last day of his term?

HILLARY: He does the symbolic walk to leave the White House the final time...

CHELSEA: But wait!

LINDA: Where's the First Lady?

BETTY: She already took a red-eye to Paris?

HILLARY: That's pretty good.

LINDA: No, you put your things in a U-Haul the night before...

HILLARY: Yes! And tie it up to the limo...

BETTY: Then / just as –

CHELSEA: He's walking towards the helicopter / and –

HILLARY: And then I drive –

LINDA: You light up a cigarette...

HILLARY: Very good, I light up a cigarette and drive across the White House lawn, Thelma and Louise, right past the press pool...

CHELSEA: Burst through the gates, and head straight back to Arkansas.

HILLARY: Yes. No! I fucking hate Arkansas. I want to live in, in... Where do I want to live?

She looks around.

Not this place. These Martha's Vineyards, these New England havens whose natural beauty has been totally obscured by their monarchical stench, from their Kennedys and Bushes and now *us*. How did I become one of those?

Deep sigh.

I tethered myself to an undisciplined man, that was my mistake.

She sits there a few beats.

Maybe I'll be a lesbian. Shack up with a stout butch who runs her own bait shop. We'll go crabbing and drink beers in our cabin and we'll stink of the sea. Chelsea can be with us, and we'll bring her into womanhood the right way.

She looks back out to the water.

CHELSEA: He's returning from his jog

BETTY: Walking up the grass towards the house

HILLARY: Fat fuck.

CHELSEA: The dog sniffs at you, tail wagging

BETTY: Looking for affection

HILLARY: For a moment, he looks like he's about to ask me something. But then he lowers his hat and whistles for his companion and they go into their dog house. So I go back to my planning.

> *A phone rings.*
>
> *MONICA and LINDA on a call.*

LINDA: Are you really planning to do this?

MONICA: I don't have a choice.

LINDA: There are ways to be protected, Monica, perjuring yourself doesn't / have to be –

MONICA: I'm not – Linda I'm not going to *perjure* myself, I –

LINDA: Is that what they told you?

MONICA: It's not perjury, it's it's the lawyer said it's a lot of 'I might have, but I don't remember', 'It's possible, but I don't remember'.

LINDA: And you're putting that in an affidavit?

MONICA: Linda what else can I *do*?!

LINDA: You can tell them the truth!

MONICA: No, this is the plan, the way to protect him, so that once he's out of office...

LINDA: Jesus.

MONICA: Then we can be together, because –

LINDA: *(Outburst.)* I've been subpoenaed too!

> *Beat.*

MONICA: What?

LINDA: I just got it.

MONICA: Oh my god. Because they know we're friends?

LINDA: I don't know.

MONICA: Do you think they're going to ask you about me? That means someone's talking, or or that they know more than we –

LINDA: Monica I don't know!

MONICA: Well what are you going to say? If they ask you about me?

LINDA: What do you think I should say?

MONICA: I think you probably don't remember a lot.

LINDA: I can't lie under oath…

MONICA: No one is asking you / to –

LINDA: Oh come on! And even if we did that, and kept this from going public, what happens after? Once we're no longer useful to them?

MONICA: I don't know.

LINDA: Me either!

MONICA: They wouldn't do anything –

LINDA: You don't know that! We're a threat to them, Monica, that is what we exist as right now, so it can't just be about your *feelings*!

> *Beat.*

Sorry.

MONICA: No…

LINDA: This is too much for the phone, I can't –

MONICA: I know.

LINDA: You want to meet for a drink?

MONICA: Yeah.

LINDA: Can we do that? Let's talk about this in person.

MONICA: Will you consider what I'm asking? Please?

LINDA: I'll consider anything that'll protect you.

MONICA: Thank you. I know it's a huge thing to ask, but…

Getting overwhelmed.

I'd be indebted to you for life. I'd do anything. Because even though he's being so terrible right now, and won't talk to me, and this is all so unbearable, I know in my inner-mind, Linda, *he loves me.*

A long silence.

LINDA: Let's meet for a drink, okay?

HILLARY raises a glass and looks at it.

She begins drying it with a dish towel, as CHELSEA appears behind her.

CHELSEA: I can do the dishes.

HILLARY: It's okay, I felt like it.

CHELSEA: So something can feel clean?

They share a tight little smile.

CHELSEA stands next to her and they do the dishes together.

HILLARY: Sorry we couldn't have Matthew come.

CHELSEA: Oh… I'm not.

HILLARY: Why, would this be a strange time for your boyfriend to get to know your family?

They laugh.

CHELSEA: I don't think we're um…anymore.

HILLARY: Oh.

CHELSEA: He's been avoiding me. Ever since this all…

HILLARY nods.

I asked Dad about it the other day, you know to like   get a guy's opinion. And he said, 'Sounds like Matthew isn't cut out for it.' I didn't get what he meant, but then   I couldn't sleep last night, and I started thinking about that game we used to play? Where you'd have me pretend to be Dad, giving a speech, and you guys would say every mean thing to me you could think of? To show me how they'll come after us? I realized Matthew never had that growing up.

Beat.

I used to cry every time. But you'd calm me down, and take my hand, and promise me that eventually I'd gain mastery over my emotions.

HILLARY sets down the dish in her hand and cries.

Really cries.

They stand like that a few beats.

HILLARY: I'm so sorry.

CHELSEA: He's been crying too.

HILLARY: *(Cry-laughing.)* Oh good!

HILLARY lets out a big breath.

CHELSEA: What are you going to do?

HILLARY shrugs at her.

They sit there a beat.

You know what popped into my head? When you guys got married, she was two.

Beat.

Sorry.

Suddenly.

The thing I – What *outcome* did they think was going to happen?

HILLARY: Sometimes you don't think about that.

CHELSEA: Then that's deluding yourself.

HILLARY: Yeah. Yeah. But I did too.

Beat.

I'm so hardened by the false things we've been accused of that I can't see the true ones. And I really should've.

CHELSEA: You shouldn't have had to.

HILLARY: That doesn't matter for us.

> *A beat.*

CHELSEA: Mom, why do you always say 'us'? Like in that game, 'This is how they'll come after us'?

HILLARY: Because   we always talked about being in this together. No matter whose name is on the door. Remember in the campaign? If you vote Clinton, you get two for the price of one?

CHELSEA: *(A beat.)* Yeah.

HILLARY: Why?

CHELSEA: Nothing.

> *MONICA crosses the stage towards LINDA.*

BETTY: You meet her at the Ritz-Carlton.

LINDA: Sweetie…

> *They hug.*

Let me buy you a drink.

> *They start to walk towards a table, but BETTY appears in front of her as an FBI agent.*

BETTY AS FBI AGENT: Ma'am, I'm going to need you to come with me.

MONICA: Who are / you?

BETTY AS FBI AGENT: *(Flashing a badge.)* FBI.

MONICA: What?

BETTY AS FBI AGENT: This way.

> *She leads her away.*

MONICA: Linda…?

> *BETTY AS FBI AGENT takes her to a table with a stack of cassette tapes on it, and when they sit we shift into a dark cramped room.*

MONICA: They take me into a room. A stack of cassette tapes on the table. Every. single. one. of our conversations. She recorded all of them.

BETTY AS FBI AGENT: Tomorrow morning the President will be deposed in the Paula Jones investigation...

MONICA: The confessions the details the sobbing...

LINDA: For your own good.

BETTY AS FBI AGENT: ...and he'll be asked about his relationship with you...

LINDA: Because you couldn't see the net you'd walked yourself into.

BETTY AS FBI AGENT: You submitted a written affidavit denying / a sexual relationship with the President...

MONICA: That's not your decision to make!

LINDA: You wanted me to lie under oath *to save a man*!

MONICA: To save a / President!

BETTY AS FBI AGENT: So we're putting an immunity deal on the table.

LINDA: You don't even see him as the President, he's some fucked-up Mr. Darcy / fantasy that you've –

MONICA: There is a special place in hell for women who don't help other women!

HILLARY: *(Whipping over to MONICA.)* Don't you fucking quote Madeleine Albright!

BETTY AS FBI: This deal has an expiration date.	MONICA: I'll quote who I want! None of you have a / monopoly on how to be a woman!

LINDA: You see this like a *game*, like you're star-crossed fucking –

MONICA: Oh I'm the one who sees it / as a game?!

HILLARY: You *both* default to games, while some of us are /
trying to *govern*!

LINDA: We're talking about a *serial predator*!

BETTY: *(Breaking FBI character.)* Okay that's a bit much.

MONICA: And what does that / have to do with me? With
ruining my life?

BETTY: Indiscretions aren't the same as / predatory —

LINDA: Go tell Paula Jones it's a bit much! Go tell Juanita /
Broaderick!

BETTY: This isn't about that! And considering he had young
women fawning over him at / every step of his career —

MONICA: I wasn't *fawning* over/ him!

HILLARY: NONE of you / actually know what you're talking
about.

LINDA: Really? I can play you back the phone calls if you
need to / jog your memory.

MONICA: Who fucking does that? Who *records* her friend's
phone calls?

BETTY: Republicans do!   HILLARY: Hate him as much
                                           / as you want, but

LINDA: Oh let's always make it about Republicans! I was just
trying to expose the truth!

BETTY: Bitch, you were trying to get a book deal!

HILLARY: When you spit hyperbole like 'predator' you're
impeaching *my* integrity!

LINDA: Yes I am, Hill/ary! Yes I am!

MONICA: Oh it's about your victimhood, how / surprising.

HILLARY: It's not *about* victimhood, it's about distinguishing
his failings from *mine*.

MONICA: And your only failing was not keeping him satisfied.

> *CHELSEA throws a plate to the ground and it shatters.*

They all look over.

CHELSEA: You want to know what my perspective was?
This. This is what I saw. The four of you, clawing, and
conniving, and deceiving each other...because of *him.* And
he's my father, and I love him, but I say this to you: he has
embarrassed all of you. He, and his men, have made fools
of you, in your desperate clamoring for the scraps of their
power. *They love this!*

>*She turns to HILLARY.*

'Two-for-one?' Ask yourself, truly, was that 'us' *ever* going
to be reciprocal?

>*She glares at her a few beats, then turns to BETTY.*

You can get back to it now.

>*She leaves.*

>*The four of them stand there a beat, avoiding each other.*

>*BETTY clears her throat and becomes the FBI agent
again.*

BETTY AS FBI AGENT: Cooperate, or you'll be charged with
perjury. Twenty-seven years in federal prison. Give us the
dress...and it all goes away.

>*BETTY leaves.*

LINDA: Maybe you'll never see it this way...but I did it to save
you.

>*MONICA laughs; small at first, but then it grows.*

MONICA: Save me? You think you saved me from something?

>*Flashbulbs go off as there's an explosion of projections
or voices:*

BETTY: DRUDGE REPORT, BLOCKBUSTER STORY:

CHELSEA: 23-YEAR-OLD, SEX RELATIONSHIP / WITH
PRESIDENT

BETTY: ...sexually involved with the love of her / life, the
President of the United States...

CHELSEA: The young intern wrote / long love letters…

BETTY: …frequent visitor to the White / House after midnight…

LINDA: …dozens of hours of phone recordings / with…

CHELSEA: …detailing the salacious love affair to / friend Linda Tripp…

LINDA: *ABC* / reports

BETTY: According to / *The Washington Post*

CHELSEA: The *National Enquirer* / has learned

LINDA: the former White House intern is –

CHELSEA: Monica / Lewinsky.

BETTY: Monica Lewin/sky.

LINDA: Monica Lewinsky.

> *MONICA covers herself from blinding light and sound.*
>
> *It disappears, and in its wake we find HILLARY.*

HILLARY: Was the 'us' ever going to be reciprocal.
That's what she asks me.
And   I don't know. But what does it matter now?

> *Beat.*

I stand there in the kitchen thinking about it. Because if I'm going to leave the 'us', I guess I need to remember who I am without it.
But I don't.
How did I get here?

> *She thinks for several beats.*

(Trying to see the memories.) Yale Law School…
I'm in the library. I'm studying. And he's looking at me across the room.
So we introduce ourselves.

> *Beat.*

I'm interning: Senate subcommittee, child custody cases…
Campaigning in Connecticut, campaigning for McGovern…
And he asks me to marry him.
I say no. I laugh.
So then working: Staff attorney for Children's Defense Fund.
Advisor for House Judiciary Committee during Watergate.
He asks me again. *No.*
A Democratic consultant calls me, tells me I'm a fresh face,
sees a future for me. Maybe congresswoman…maybe even
President…
And he asks me one more time, 'cause now he's moving to
Arkansas to run for Congress.

> *Struggling.*

Then what happens?

> *Remembering.*

I take the bar in both places.
In Arkansas, I pass. In Washington, I fail. And that one
failure…
I say yes.
I go with him. And begin two decades of being a First Lady.
I'm thirty-one.

> *She looks around the space.*

I'm tired of these memories.

> *She forces herself to stay in it.*

I can hear the ocean. And I realize the kitchen's gotten dark.
It would feel incredible to leave.
To let go of this need to chip away at progress. This insane
fusion of self-abasement and self-flagellation and self-
aggrandizement that we call *politics*. It would feel   good.
But wouldn't it also mean that it's all been in service of him?

> *Long beat.*

Reciprocal…

> *Lets the word echo out.*

What would that even look like?

Tries to picture it.

It would have to be small. I'd have to moderate.

Arriving at a conclusion.

And I'd have to stay with him.

MONICA appears.

HILLARY and MONICA notice each other.

They realize there's no one else in the space with them except THE SAXOPHONIST. (And maybe he's even stepped out for now.)

They let this be awkward for a moment.

Then another moment.

Then MONICA looks back at her.

MONICA: Do you want to hear something weird?

HILLARY looks at her. Turns and looks behind her to make sure she's not talking to someone else, then turns back.

HILLARY: What?

MONICA: I'm thinking through the big political sex scandals. The Eliot Spitzer Scandal. The Mark Foley Scandal. The John Edwards Scandal...

HILLARY: The David Petraeus Scandal.

MONICA: The Strom Thurmond Scandal.

HILLARY: The Ted Kennedy Scandal.

MONICA: The David Vitter Scandal.

HILLARY: The Larry Craig Scandal.

MONICA: The Gary Condit Scandal.

HILLARY: The John Ensign Scandal.

MONICA: The Mark Sanford Scandal.

HILLARY: The Anthony Weiner Scandal.

MONICA: The Al Franken Scandal.

HILLARY: The Donald Trump Scandal*s*.

MONICA: The Bob Livingston Scandal, the Dennis Hastert Scandal, the Newt Gingrich Scandal. Also known as...

HILLARY: The three Republican Speakers of the House during our second term.

MONICA: The guys who led the impeachment efforts.

HILLARY: Yep.

> *They smile at each other.*
>
> *They're surprised to find themselves smiling at each other.*

Why were you thinking about that?

MONICA: Because this gets called the Monica Lewinsky Scandal.

> *Beat.*

You made sure everyone knew my name.

HILLARY: You think I did that?

MONICA: They knew my name, and they sure found ways to get in touch – thanks for unleashing the internet, by the way.

> *Beat.*

You'll judge this, but I waited for him to defend me. I was sure he would, 'cause I had played by all the rules, and did everything they asked. 'I might've but I don't remember', 'It's possible, but I don't remember'. But that's not what happens. When I turn on the TV at my lowest, contemplating the worst, what I hear is not a defense, not a reward for my loyalty. It's just nine words: 'I did not have sexual relations with *that woman.*'

> *Beat.*

Sneering at the camera, *you don't exist.* Pointing for the country, that-a-way, there's your prey. I hear those words, and an immense question drops on me: Was any of it ever real? Had he ever even... Because here was the beginning of you two turning me into the scapegoat...

HILLARY: Well...

MONICA: The crazy one, the stalker. 'Narcissistic loony toon' I think you called me.

HILLARY: Listen…

MONICA: *That woman.*

HILLARY: Monica, I might've had more sympathy if you hadn't fucked my husband.

They share another look.

MONICA: I'm sure my time here's almost up. And then I'll sink back to whatever pocket of your memory I occupy. But I have to ask: You talk about all this as though it was the worst thing to ever happen to you…

HILLARY: I'd say second worst.

MONICA: Sure. Well this whole Martha's Vineyard story? How it made you wonder if it's your turn now – because he owed it to you?

HILLARY: What about it?

MONICA: I'm trying to think of the exact timeline, but you must have known by then that he was going to get impeached. You knew the Senate would never kick him out, he wouldn't have to resign in disgrace, but the House was going to serve him two articles of impeachment anyway: perjury and obstruction of justice. Those House Republicans went after you two with *everything.*

HILLARY: They did.

MONICA: It really was a vast right-wing conspiracy.

HILLARY: It really was.

MONICA: My question is: What was happening to the poll numbers?

HILLARY: That's your question? The American people didn't like seeing their President get attacked for –

MONICA: *Your* poll numbers.

Beat.

As you sat on that beach, what was happening to them?

HILLARY: I was the wronged woman.

MONICA: So was I, but we'll set that aside a moment. Do you remember? I think you do. Ten points. You climbed ten points, to sixty-seven percent, the highest it had ever been, and ever would be, in your entire career. So…second worst thing to ever happen to you?

HILLARY: You think this made it *easier* to launch a political career?

MONICA: I do.

HILLARY: People love to say how this all backfired for Republicans, how it hurt *their* negatives, not the administration's – but when they say that, they mean for *him*. No one ever bothered to measure how the stain of it might stay with me; how it might make people *feel* like I'm corrupt, or untrustworthy, even if they can't quite put their finger on why. *Those* are the poll numbers it affected!

MONICA: Still.
Like it or not…
I birthed your political career.

> *They stare at each other again.*
>
> *HILLARY looks at her in appraisal of something.*

HILLARY: You said you wondered if any of it was real. With him.

MONICA: Yeah…

HILLARY: 'Long enough have you dream'd contemptible dreams,
Now I wash the gum from your eyes,
You must habit yourself to the dazzle of the light
and of every moment of your life.'

> *Beat.*

It's from *Leaves of Grass*. The book Bill gave me after our first date.

> *MONICA softly shatters.*
>
> *They sit there in silence.*
>
> *HILLARY goes to the blue dress.*

> *Picks it up and takes it back over to MONICA.*
>
> *Offers it.*

You hold the blue dress in your hands

> *MONICA looks at the dress.*
>
> *Takes it in her arms.*
>
> *She looks back up at HILLARY.*

MONICA: You sit there by the beach

HILLARY: And you think about the choice in front of you

MONICA: And you think about the choice in front of you

HILLARY: You know, now, it's either your welfare or his

MONICA: Either your career or his

HILLARY: You just hope you still have the courage

MONICA: Something to offer

HILLARY: That you haven't given up too much of yourself

MONICA: That you haven't already missed your moment

> *The others have appeared around them.*

BETTY: Bill comes back from his morning jog…

MONICA: You throw him his first bone

HILLARY: Bill…

MONICA: You say

HILLARY: I'm thinking about life after the White House.

BETTY: He stops in his tracks

LINDA: *(To MONICA.)* You walk into the concrete building

HILLARY: Holding the bag with the dress in your arms

LINDA: And you ignore all the faces sneaking glances

> *MONICA rises to her feet.*

BETTY: Chelsea comes out of the house

CHELSEA: I see you talking, and offer to go somewhere / else

HILLARY: No.

MONICA: you say

HILLARY: Stay.

CHELSEA: There's a new energy between you

HILLARY: You're in the elevator, Monica

LINDA: You're gripping the bag tighter

MONICA: Bill's naming off districts and state houses

CHELSEA: Advisers he could get on the phone

MONICA: Chelsea is smiling

CHELSEA: Dad seeing the path of his redemption laid out in front of him

HILLARY: The elevator doors open

LINDA: The agents are waiting

MONICA: Bill snaps

BETTY: New York Senate

MONICA: he says

BETTY: Moynihan's about to announce his retirement.

CHELSEA: I say I love New York.

HILLARY: You step out of the elevator

MONICA: And you say

HILLARY: Stop.

MONICA crosses the stage, dress in her arms.

Before we talk about this any further, something needs to be absolutely clear. Because of her, because of this...they'll be after us like never before. Checking every syllable. Spinning every action we take, however noble, towards scandal. So if we do this...we have to become *disciplined.* Every press release. Every interview. Every meeting. Every intern. Meticulously coordinated. Your way was your way, but this will have to be mine now. Do you understand?

CHELSEA: He warns you:

BETTY: It'll make you look calculating. And cold. And people won't trust you.

CHELSEA: You say

HILLARY: I don't have a choice

LINDA: But of course she does.

BETTY: But of course she doesn't.

HILLARY: I don't know if I can ever just...be. I'll try. I'll work very, very hard. Harder than anyone else. And I think, over time, people will see me. I think they'll realize why I've had to be the way I've had to be. As a woman. As a Clinton. And then maybe I can do something important.

> *MONICA has reached the edge of the stage.*
>
> *She looks out.*

BETTY: The agent greets you

LINDA: Sees you and the dress, and says

BETTY: You're doing the right thing.

CHELSEA: And you say

MONICA: I don't have a choice.

BETTY: But of course she does.

LINDA: But of course she doesn't.

> *MONICA looks at the dress in her arms a moment, then lets it fall and disappear.*
>
> *THE SAXOPHONIST's song ends.*
>
> *MONICA turns back to HILLARY.*

MONICA: How does it end?

HILLARY: Bill takes my hand and says okay.

Then Chelsea says okay.

Then I say okay.

MONICA: And then you say

HILLARY: Let's get to work.

BLACKOUT.

73